This Spinning Planet

Mary Zeoli

BookLeaf Publishing

Presentation by *BookLeaf Publishing*

Web: www.bookleafpub.com

E-mail: info@bookleafpub.com

ISBN: 9789357616447

First edition 2022

PREFACE

This collection of poems and prose are a small attempt to make sense of the unexplainable chaos of life, love and our own choices.
It is filled with stories of things that have already come to pass, moments that remain entirely in our heads and the quiet, tiny fears that may never happen.

Come,
Stay a while,
Sit with these thoughts and catch your breath.

Nor you or I
Can slow this spinning planet,
But oh, how we try.

Rise or Fall

The light of day uncovers all; and all our faults.

Will you hide or rise?

I hope you have the courage to choose.

Neither Shall You

At the bus stop - eyes glimmering and rheumy.

He told me once,

The rivers do not slow, for fear of overflowing.

For fear of taking up space, the mountain does not move.

Neither shall you.

My Heart is a Home

My Heart is a Home.
I have known that it is patient.

There have been hesitant footsteps,
And brave booming knocks, for which the door
would not open.

For a while, even visitors who thought they
would stay.

They came with bags and bags; their memories
and quirks.

When they left.
You were there to unpack it all.

The home was once bigger.
It was comfortable and the door was open,
swung freely on its hinges.

It was made warm by summer days, bare feet
and laughter.
It rested behind bone bars in your chest and on
those excellent days, it grew and hummed.

Little by little, your body grew up but the home
got smaller and smaller.
Heartbreak was an unkind and noisy neighbour.

One day soon, Your Home will remember how it
felt to be big and brave
and warm and proud.

Welcome, it will say quietly.

Welcome.

This Spinning Planet

5

And my time on this Earth has not prepared me,
for running an
unwinnable race.

Fireflies

There is an emptiness,
A cavernous feeling

I am shaking.
I am shuddering.

No matter the darkness,
There are fireflies here.

Screaming Planet.

The Earth feels within,

I am a screaming planet

Nothing is left here.

Tick, Tick, Tick.

Three.
I am little
I can taste summer on my tongue.
Time stretches ahead like a long red string; tied
to something I cannot see.

Six.
Half-way there.
I am keeping count.
Time ticks like a metronome and flows like a
river.

Twelve.

Time reads life like a book.
Happy memories are dog-eared and tattered.
Watermarked, ripped, bookmarked and loved.

Time has served me well.

;

Sometimes grief is so loud, there is nothing left
but silence.

Woman is a Witch.

Woman is a Witch.
She feels more than most,

The almost imperceptible change in air,
The warm hug of a host.

Woman is a Witch,
Labelled as a sin, an unholy host,

Born of maiden descendants fair.
An all-knowing eye and power engrossed.

Woman is a Witch,
Her burden alone.

The Space Between

There are three here, but one should not be.

There is you,
  and me
  and the space between.

It is the disappointing silence between lover's
platitudes.
The ache of want; for something that cannot
exist.
It is the look that lingers, waiting to be seen and
heard.
It is the slowing of the heart-beat that once raced
forward.
It is the painful tip-toe dance around what once
was there, and now is not.

There are three here,
It is me that should not be

Lessons From the Trees

Stand tall, dear Oak.
Stand proud, stand brave.

Do not bow like the willows that weep.
For they only bring solace
to the crying and the meek.

Stand tall, dear Oak.
You were not built like the Rowan or the Ash.
Born out myth;
To be danced under in moonlight but forbidden
to brash.

Stand proud, dear Oak.
You are the watchful, the patient and wise.
Present and bold.

Do not shy from your duty.
Condemned and blessed with a life, long lived.

Unknown Magic

You were born of fire and brimstone

I suppose no one ever told you,
That the same fire,
The one that destroys
Also creates.

Which will you choose?

A Day, A Month, A Year

August,
The loudest name and the longest month.
Filled with the promise of new.

I can't fight the cold, my darling.
Not when it's me against you.
December is next.
God, I hope I make it till then.

Sixteen Again.

I have a weakness for bubble tea and dinosaurs.
I think red hair is amazing.

Poetry, books and small furry creatures are what
make me happy.
It takes me five minutes to cook two-minute
noodles.
I have a new favourite word each week
not intentionally
It just happens,

I have a very strange train of thought.
I often find myself saying things that have no
relevance whatsoever to anyone.
My poor grammar is compensated by the fact
that I apparently write good poetry.

But I bet that's a lie.

Letters to Nowhere

I write and write, but never read out.
I pour out my fears onto safety.
Bland white paper.

A changeling to start again; to erase and
re-write.

Life passes in a circle,
In an ouroboros loop of seasons.

Somehow in the middle though, we get older.
Then it begins again,
And a new lesson is learnt.

The Missing Piece

What happens when a person breaks?
Are they thrown away
Or taken and fixed?

Would they take out the stuffing and fluff the
fur?
Like the Teddy Bear from when I was three.

He never did come back the same,
The space inside, where his chest should be,
Was a little more hollow
but only I could tell.

Balloon Thoughts

She lies on her bed.
Stares at the ceiling,
Questions float around in her head like helium
balloons.
She plucks one down and begins to wonder

"How many others have stared at this ceiling
too?"
"How many have questioned themselves?"
"And how many times were the answers clear?"

She thinks, long into the night
Yet the only answer she can find
Is wrapped in another conundrum.

"How many were like me,
Lost and afraid to try?"

"Millions, I suppose"

Waiting Game

Love is a waiting game,

I wish I could tell you that strawberry skin and
cherry kisses do not sour,

Sometimes they age like plums and wine.
They stain, deep, dark and red.

and take years to fade.